Alfred's Premier Piano Course

Pop /

Dennis Alexander • Gayle Kowalchyk • E. L. Lancaster • Victoria McArthur • Martha Mier

Alfred's *Premier Piano Course* Pop and Movie Hits Book 2A includes familiar pieces that reinforce concepts included in Lesson Book 2A. The music continues the strong pedagogical focus of the course while providing the enjoyment of playing familiar popular music. Duet accompaniments, when included, create rich sounds and can aid the student with rhythmic security. Both solo and duet parts contain measure numbers for easy reference.

The pieces in this book correlate page-by-page with the materials in Lesson Book 2A. They should be assigned according to the instructions in the upper right corner of each page of this book. They also may be assigned as review material at any time after the student has passed the designated Lesson Book page. Pop and Movie Hits 2A also can be used to supplement any beginning piano method.

Allowing students to study music they enjoy is highly motivating. Consequently, reading and rhythm skills often improve greatly when studying pop and movie music. The authors hope that the music in Pop and Movie Hits 2A brings hours of enjoyment.

Edited by Morton Manus

Produced by
Alfred Music Publishing Co., Inc.
P.O. Box 10003
Van Nuys, CA 91410-0003
alfred.com

Printed in USA.

ISBN-10: 0-7390-6689-7

ISBN-13: 978-0-7390-6689-8

CONTENTS

Use with Alfred's Premier Piano Course
Lesson Book 2A, pages 4–5

Star Wars
(Main Theme)

by **JOHN WILLIAMS**

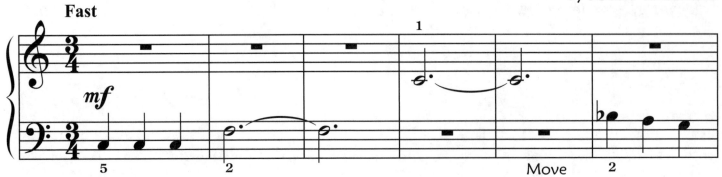

Duet: Student plays one octave higher.

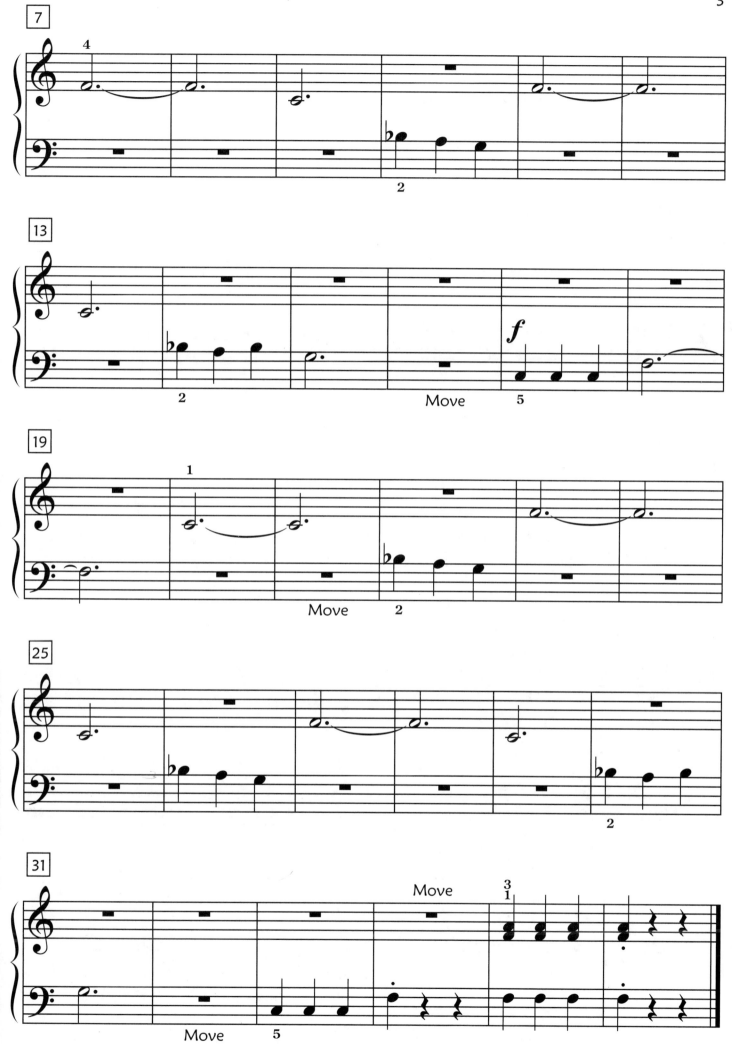

Heigh-Ho
(from *Snow White and the Seven Dwarfs*)

Words by Larry Morey
Music by Frank Churchill

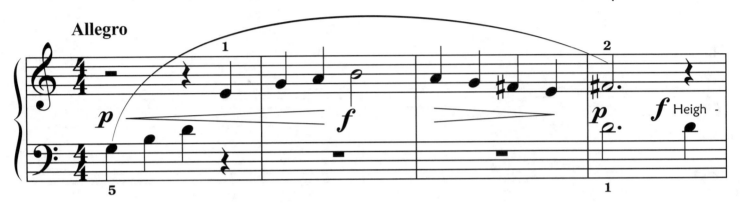

Duet: Student plays one octave higher.

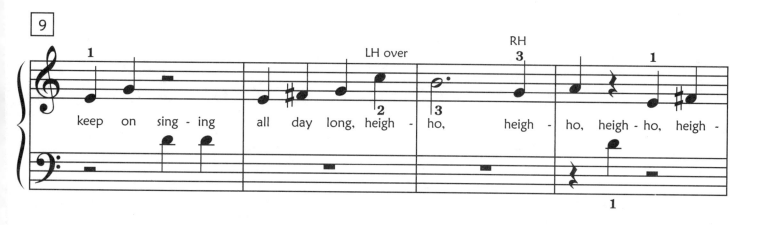

The Chicken Dance
(Dance Little Bird)

Music by
Terry Rendall and Werner Thomas
English Lyrics by Paul Parnes

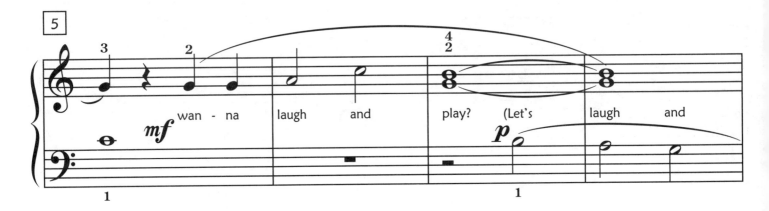

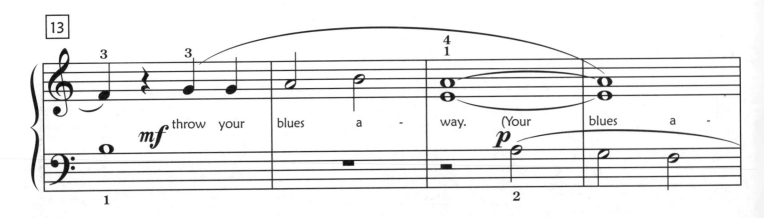

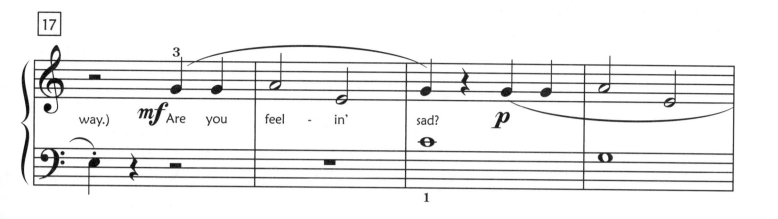

17

way.) *mf* Are you feel - in' sad? *p*

21

mf Got a prob - lem? Here's a cure. *p* (We got the

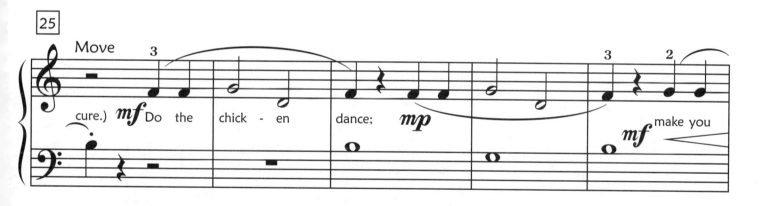

25

Move

cure.) *mf* Do the chick - en dance; *mp* *mf* make you

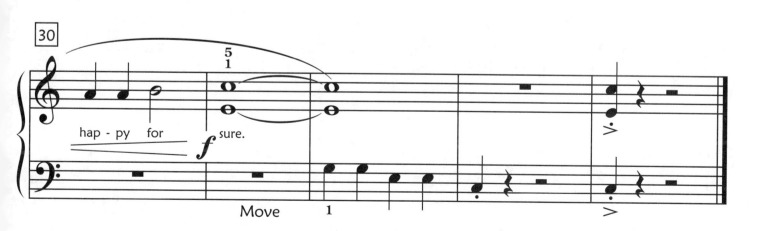

30

hap - py for *f* sure.

Move

It's My Party

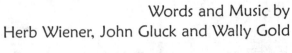

Words and Music by
Herb Wiener, John Gluck and Wally Gold

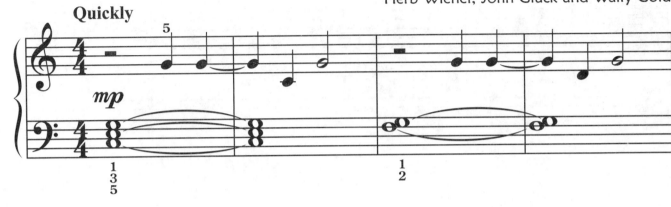

Duet: Student plays one octave higher.

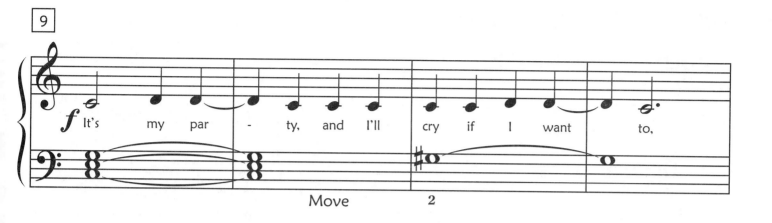

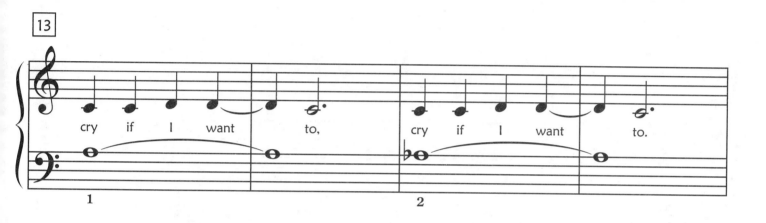

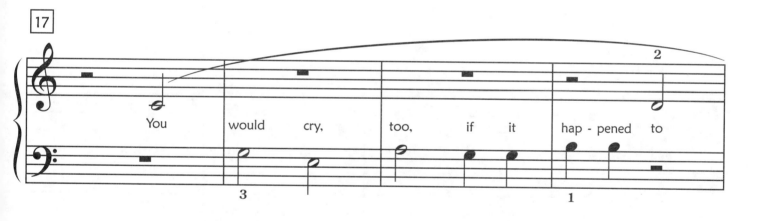

(We're Gonna) Rock Around the Clock

Words and Music by
Max C. Freedman and Jimmy De Knight

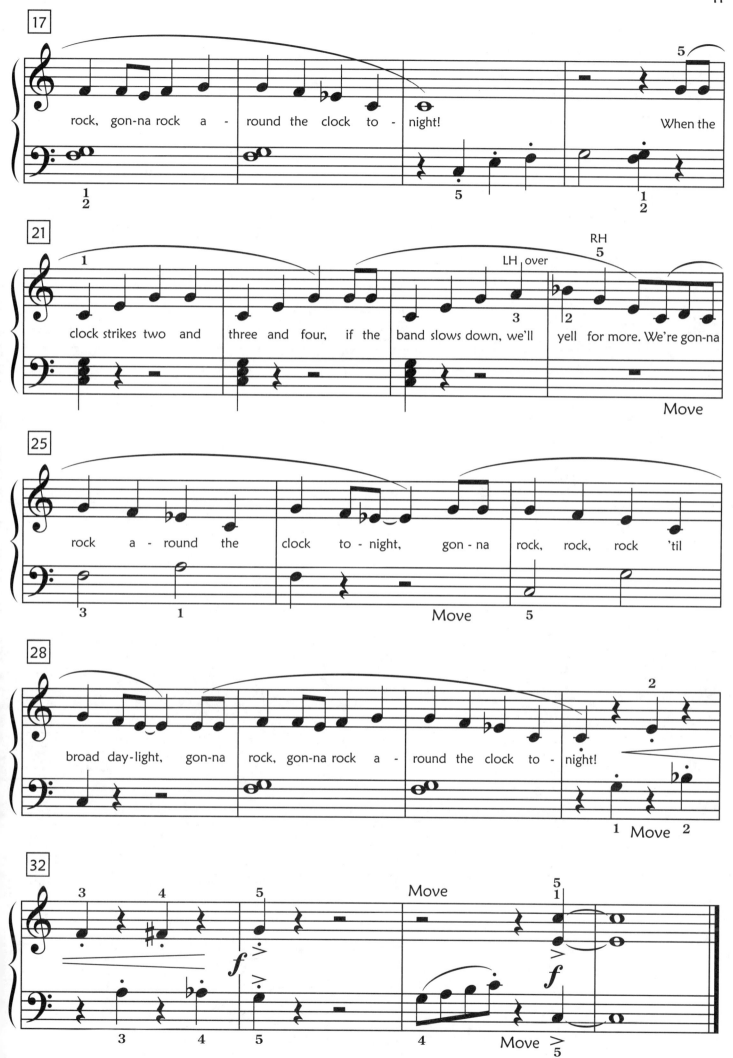

Chim Chim Cher-ee
(from Walt Disney's *Mary Poppins*)

Words and Music by
Richard M. Sherman and Robert B. Sherman

Duet: Student plays one octave higher.

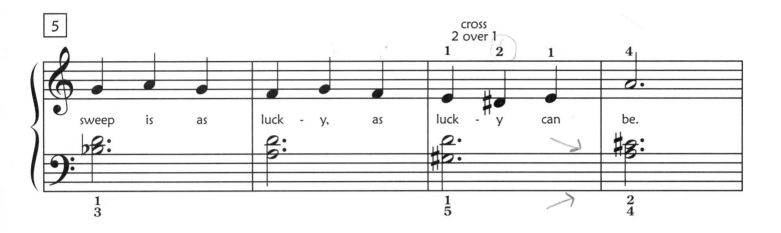

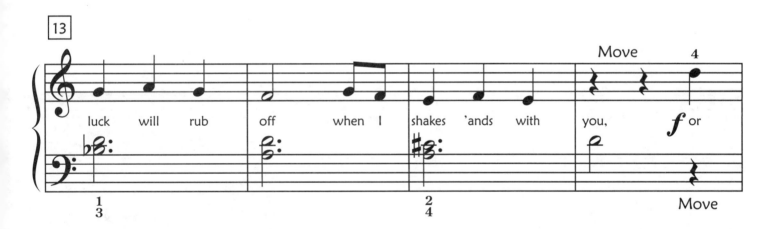

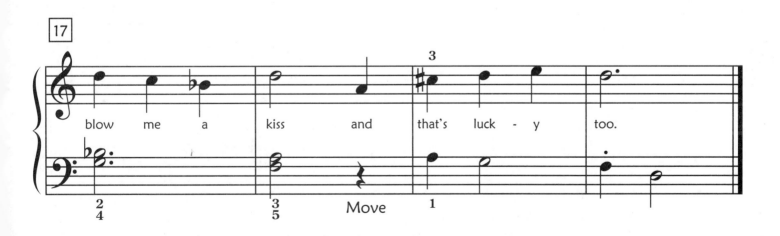

Beauty and the Beast

(from Walt Disney's *Beauty and the Beast*)

Lyrics by Howard Ashman
Music by Alan Menken

Duet: Student plays one octave higher.

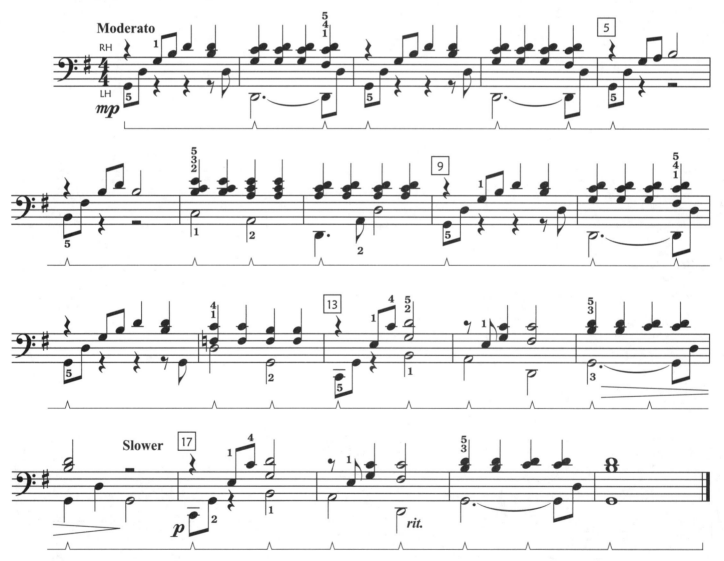

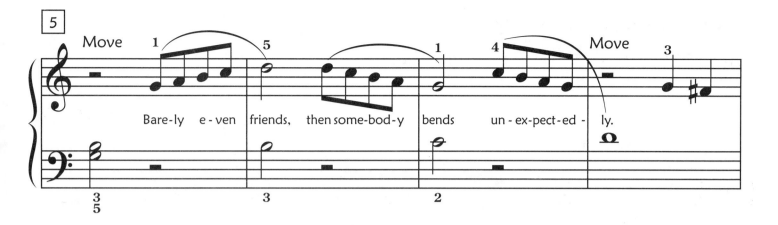

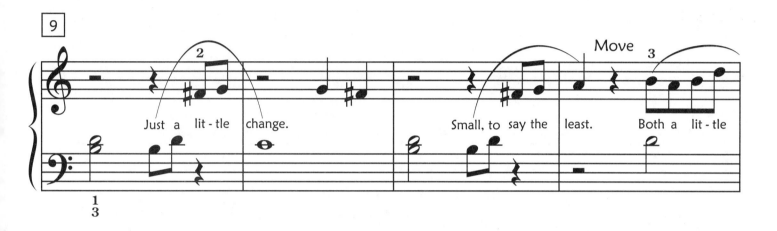

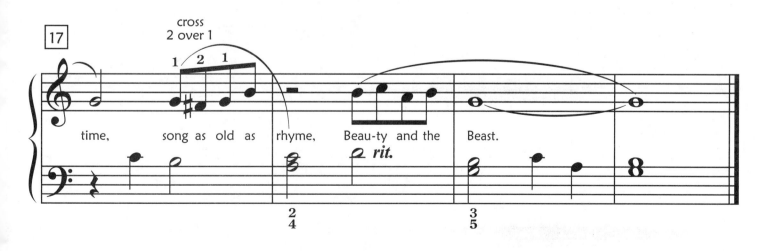

Catch a Falling Star

Words and Music by
Paul Vance and Lee Pockriss

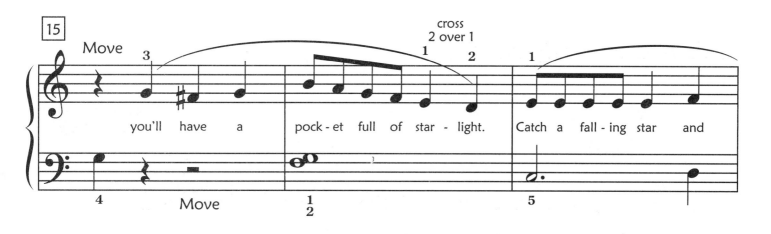

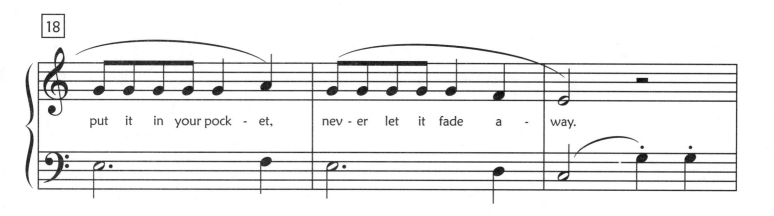

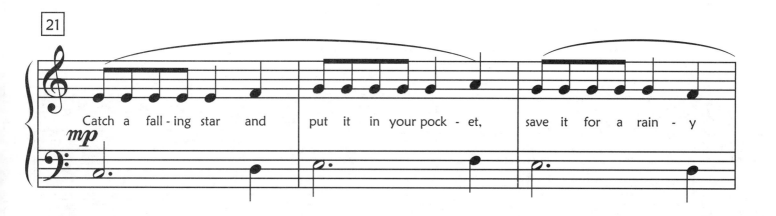

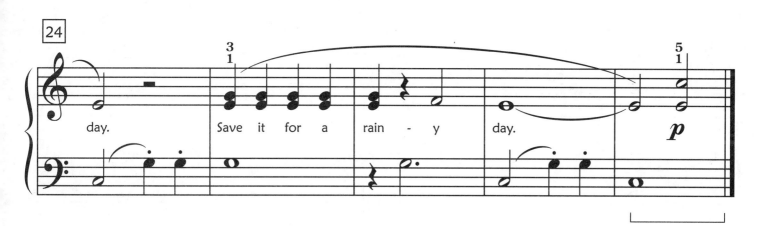

Wipe Out

by The Surfaris

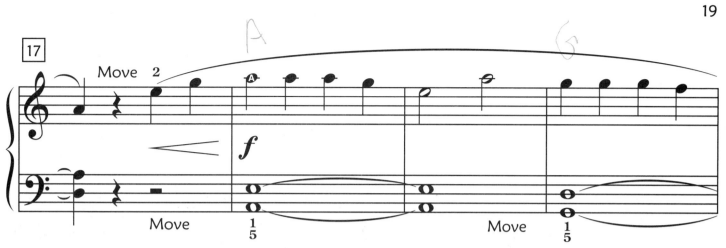

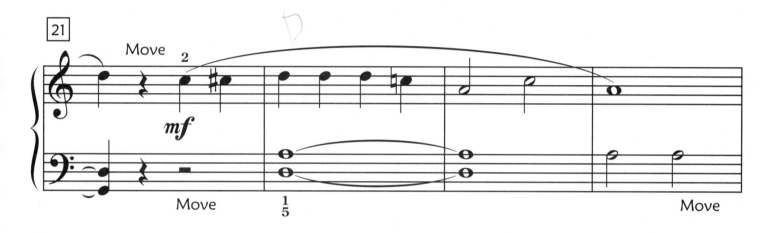

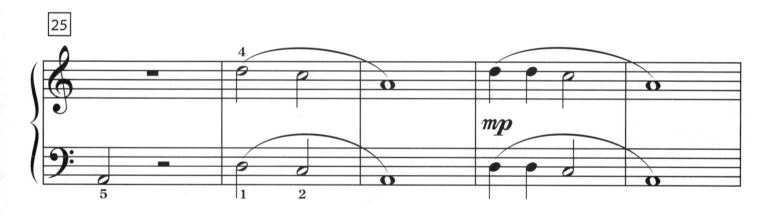

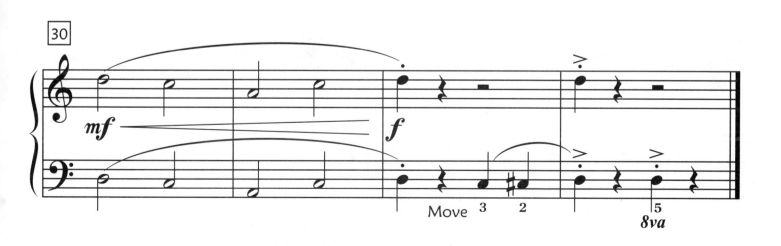

James Bond Theme

by Monty Norman

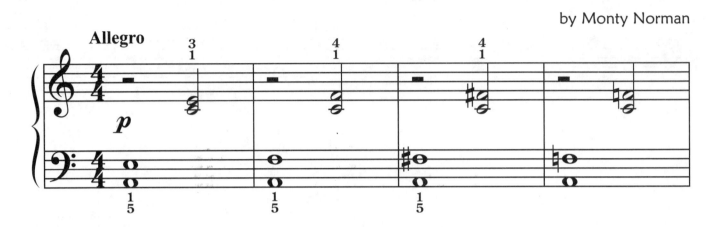

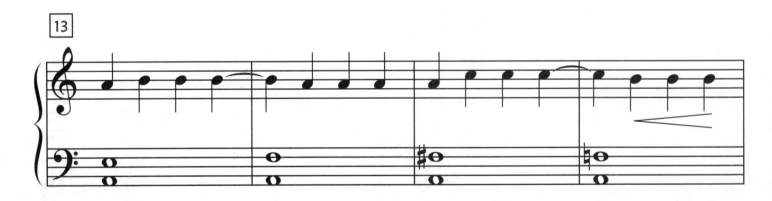

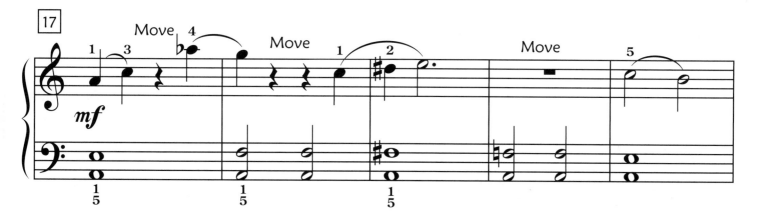

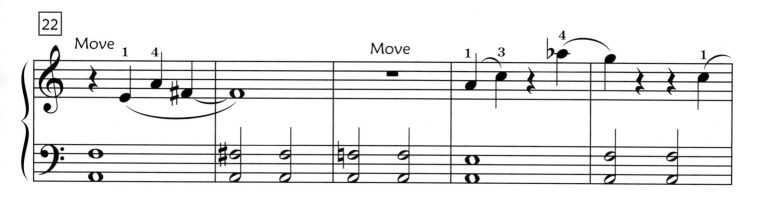

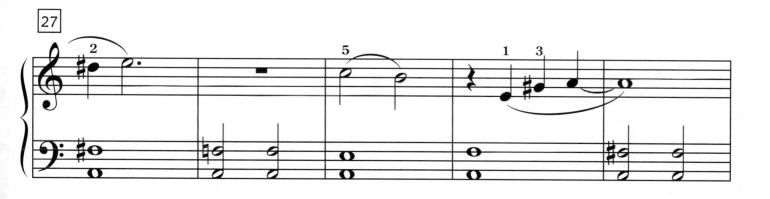

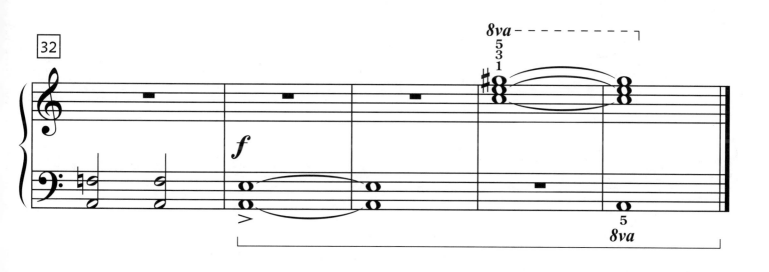

The Lion Sleeps Tonight

New Lyric and Revised Music by
George David Weiss, Hugo Peretti and Luigi Creatore

In the jun - gle, the qui - et jun - gle, the li - on sleeps to -

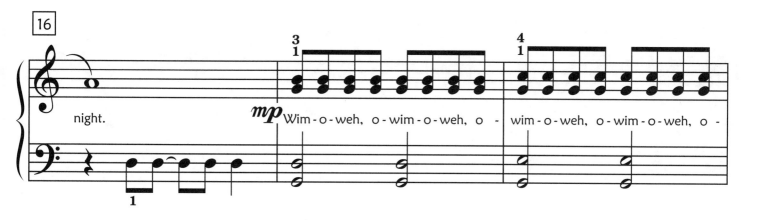

night. *mp* Wim - o - weh, o - wim - o - weh, o - wim - o - weh, o - wim - o - weh, o -

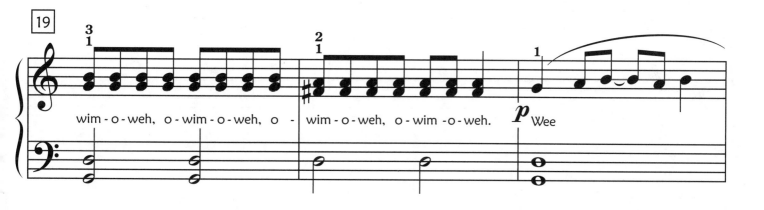

wim - o - weh, o - wim - o - weh, o - wim - o - weh, o - wim - o - weh. *p* Wee

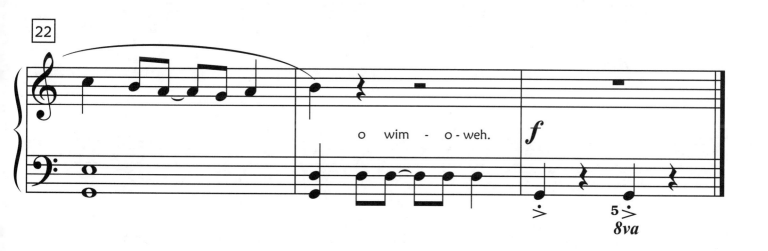

o wim - o - weh. *f*

Happy Birthday to You

Words and Music by
Mildred J. Hill and Patty S. Hill

*No pedal when performed with duet.

Duet: Student plays one octave higher.